7 Powerful Ways to Solve your Problems

A Guide to be More Efficient

By

Hina Siddiqui

DISCLAIMER

DEDICATION

To every single person and situation that has given me the reason to master the art of Problem Solving

TABLE OF CONTENTS

FOREWORD

Would you like to accept a challenge to find a single individual on this planet who doesn't have to deal with problems on a regular basis. Sounds weird? Untrue? In my life time, I haven't met anyone who avoids problems, although I have come across many who are great at solving problems when they arise.

Problems do exist, and not always in reality—but in our minds. They can be as small and ordinary as what to wear for the party tonight or as complex as getting out of a painful marriage. They can be as usual as having a disrupted water supply at your home or as abnormal as surviving a train or car crash. All of us face a variety of problems every day. Most of the time we use our own instinct to solve them, while other times we have someone's assistance.

This very short guidebook is about finding a few great ways to overcome problems and live stress free.

Let's move on….

PROBLEMS BY DEFINITIONS

What is a problem? The Concise Oxford Dictionary (1995) defines a problem as: *"A doubtful or difficult matter requiring a solution"* and *"Something hard to understand or accomplish or deal with."* Broadly the problems are the situations where it's difficult to achieve what we want to.

Few examples:

I am trying hard to quit smoking but can't

My children are not doing well in studies

My partner does not seem to love me anymore

My poor communication is proving to be an obstacle in my professional growth

I don't look good enough

Attending this meeting is extremely necessary and my car broke down

My grandmother is very difficult to adjust with

I didn't get the salary hike as I expected

Why don't people understand me?

And so on....

In various scenarios, one thing is reoccurring — the difficulty in achieving an objective. You want something and it's not happening your way. We may also divide problems into two groups. Closed Problems are where something has happened (or has not happened) without expectation. Open-ended Problems are where there are obstacles while we want to achieve a specific objective.

Whatever may be the nature of a Problem, what I like most about problems is that they are meant to be solved in some way or the other. Each problem is unique and requires a specific way of thinking to be solved. However, problem solving follows a basic pattern of identifying a problem, finding possible solutions to that problem, and then choosing the best solution and finally implementing it successfully. This is what almost each one of us knows. Although this is a vast subject that requires our most creative and logical skills to solve different problems in different situations, but within the scope of this book (as the title suggests) we shall figure out 7 ways to solve your problems to be more efficient in everything you do.

"The formulation of the problem is often more essential than its solution, which may be merely a matter of mathematical or experimental skill." — **Albert Einstein**

5

#1 Solve the Right Problem

If you've tried to solve a problem with every possible solution with little or no success, your challenge isn't finding a better solution. It's finding a better problem.

Let me give you a few examples here to help you understand. Once when I was at work, one of my team members used to reach office late; almost every day. She said she could never get up early enough in the morning despite her efforts. To fix her issue, she'd tried to set up an alarm, go to the bed earlier at night, treat insomnia – she tried everything but gained no results. She later discovered the reason to her problem after getting the symptoms of ill health. So, what may be the right problem here? Her health probably.

During the initial years of my career, I was a job hopper. I was too good at finding faults even with the perfect job situations. Every person around seemed to conspire against me for different reasons. This continued endlessly until I discovered that I had an adjustment problem. Why? Because of my poor self esteem and ever occurring self doubt.

One of my best buddies was living a bad marriage. Every time we talked, a new fault in her husband got the focus. Finally, I suggested why don't you guys get separated when you are not meant for each other and don't complement one another. The very thought scared her. We dug deeper to explore that she was actually trying to dominate him her way. So, her unrealistic expectations and dominant behavior played the culprit.

If your employee is not responsible for their work efforts, it may not be because of a lack of motivation or irresponsible behavior; they might just need training to upgrade their skills so they can perform better.

Sometimes, you really need to be brutally honest to find the root of the problems

Spend time with the problem. Stay mindful and be attentive to every aspect of it. Be extremely honest. It may be easy to throw blame on people, circumstances and situations and hard to see our own behavior and attitude as the root of the problem we are trying to solve. However, the goal here is to look for the root that needs to be attacked.

You may consider seeking help from a good friend or a close one whose opinion you trust. Stay open. Don't feel bad if you are shown an aspect that you don't like or appreciate. Focus on your EVENTUAL BENEFIT.

#2 Ignore the Problems You Cannot Help or Solve

I know that I previously said that problems are meant to be solved. But it is also true that ignoring them at times is the best solution. For example, people problems.

Can you control the way others behave? You can't. You can only control your reactions. For example, your best friend is visibly getting jealous of your recent achievement that you are so proud of. You never thought they could. You were 100% sure that they were always on your side. But what can you do? You can probably talk to them, but that might create more complications in the relationship. Or, you could decide to distance yourself from them and risk losing the friendship. You might think: what makes them a good friend even though they are behaving jealously? It's natural. We seldom exhibit temporary emotions. Simply ignoring what happened in this situation is a great thing to do, in my opinion.

Now let's see what happens if you don't ignore. You think about it, wait, overthink it. That makes you negative and negativity will conspire against your growth. So, control this behavior before it controls you.

My husband should have given me a costlier gift on our wedding anniversary.

I went out of the way to attend his birthday party but he didn't even bother to call me on my big day.

Despite our great relationship, my colleague didn't help me with the new project when I needed most.

My best friend didn't tell me about her new found love.

And the list is endless.

A major cause to our raised emotional stress levels lies in the unmet expectations from our relationships. One thing we need to understand is that every person operates according to their own mentality, priorities, goals, aspirations, moods and personality. People do things for their own reasons. Tying our happiness to what they think and do is nothing but a way too IDEALISTIC, UNREALISTIC and STUPID act of expectation. Isn't it?

#3 Elaborate the Problem

Albert Einstein quotes "If I had an hour to solve a problem, I'd spend 55 minutes thinking about the problem and 5 minutes thinking about solutions."

Prepare a statement of the problem and find someone who you trust to review it and talk about it with you. If the problem is a job situation, review it with your supervisor or the appropriate committee or resource.

Investigate the causes and circumstances that led to the creation of the problem. If the problem involves too many unanswered questions, fact-finding can prove to be much more effective than any attempt to find an immediate solution.

You may consider these questions:

- What is the problem?
- Is it my problem?
- Can I solve it? Is it worth solving?
- Is this the real problem or merely the symptom of a larger one?
- If this is an old problem, what's wrong with the previous solution?
- Does it need an immediate solution, or can it wait?
- Is it likely to go away by itself?
- Can I risk ignoring it?
- Does the problem have ethical dimensions?
- What conditions must the solution satisfy?
- Will the solution affect something that must remain unchanged?

#4 Solve with a Fresh and Positive Mindset

"We cannot solve our problems with the same thinking we used when we created them". Albert Einstein

In the normal scenario, when faced with a problem, we can automatically panic and show symptoms of intense fear, breathlessness and trembling.

"Problems are meant to be solved, but unfortunately, a lot of people choose to complain, worry, and cry about them."— **Edmond Mbiaka**

As our brain cannot multitask,

1. We can either set it to focus on problem or
2. Finding an appropriate solution.

"Which are you?"

Like many of you, for countless significant years in my life, I had been among those who dwell and fret on the problems rather than solutions. And even worse, I was worrying and worrying harder about the consequences if the problem had not been resolved.

You can easily imagine what this kind of thought pattern and behavior can land us into- "Infinite misery".

Quite later, I started looking at problems as a game rather than an excruciating process. The fun is in playing the game. If you are able to resolve it with high efficiency, you win. Don't you? And beyond that, you learn new tricks and techniques of the game. It is a pure learning experience.

View the problem as a positive challenge and as an opportunity to show off your creative skills. Many times I have observed that what I thought of as a problem later turned out to be great opportunity.

Consider taking several 5 Minute-Breaks during the Problem Solving Process

Yes. It works. Coming back to the same problem with a fresh perspective makes you more capable of seeing it from a different angle and then dealing with it better. During these 5 minute breaks, consider deviating your mind from dwelling on the problem you are trying to handle. A calm mind is more capable of understanding things.

#5 Sleep over your Problems

Are you trying to find the solution to your complex problems? Sleep over them. This works awesome, trust me. Had I not tried it for myself, I would have never shared it with you. I have often used this method to gain ideas for my books and trainings.

Since I have known the facts, functions and powers of the subconscious mind, I have tried to use it for my benefit in almost all situations. I choose my last thoughts carefully (not always, but most times), especially when I seek answers from my inner self about various things including the hard decision or even creative ideas. By doing so, I let my subconscious mind work on it because the subconscious is always at work even when we sleep. It's normal for me to wake up in the morning with either the clear solutions/answers, or an intuition.

Sleep Boosts Creativity

One study from Lancaster University that was published in the journal *Memory and Cognitive* shows that sleeping on your problems really does help people process difficult problems. Sara C. Mednick PhD, assistant professor in the department of psychiatry at the University of California, San Diego, says, "Creativity is the ability to connect disparate ideas in new and useful ways".

During the day, an area of the brain called the hippocampus takes in information and lets us hold it in our minds. It knows why you learned the information, Mednick says. For example, the hippocampus may learn that you need to turn at the red building to reach the doctor's office. During REM sleep, the hippocampus shuts down and allows the information it stored to move into the neocortex, the part of the brain that holds the sum of all of your experiences. Once a memory or experience reaches the neocortex, it can be associated with all the other memories.

And that's where creativity happens, Mednick says. The neocortex might match that shade of red on the building with the need to come up with the color for a toy, and *voilà!* Priming your brain to make these new connections seems to be key, research shows. An idea might seem to come out of nowhere, but in fact it's the end of a process that may have begun days ago.

#6 Make Yourself Less Prone to Problems

"An ounce of prevention is worth a pound of cure." Benjamin Franklin

It's worth figuring out why some people have all the luck and the rest spend their entire life finding out what they did wrong to bring them through so much pain. Once in a while, all of us have to face some serious obstacles in life. But many of us seem to struggle much more than the rest. I have heard several people say, "I don't understand why I am so unlucky".

Why does one person suffer with diabetes their entire life while another stays healthy for most of it?

Why is it that few people enjoy solid relationships while others always wonder if perfect relationships actually exist?

Why does one woman wait ardently to see one positive pregnancy strip while another woman drives a van full of kids?

I too spent many years of my life searching for answers to such questions. Then I realized after a lot of research and thought that our attitude is mainly responsible for many things in our life. An anxious person, having all the fears and doubts about themselves and the world, is more likely to attract problems than those who stay calm and positive.

Here are a few things that keep me in good mind:

- Staying happy with a positive state of mind where I chose my thoughts and respective actions
- Believing in myself
- Building on healthy and powerful habits
- Taking every challenge as an opportunity
- Staying focused and organized
- Keeping good intentions towards everyone and wishing prosperity everywhere and for everyone
- Disciplining myself

You may consider downloading my book "Road To Riches Of Life" which talks about it in detail.

#7 Prevent Further Problems

"Passive inactivity, because you have not been given specific instructions to do this or to do that, is a serious deficiency." — *George C. Marshall*

As most of us indulge in the habit of procrastination, we postpone our problems to be solved later. Even after gaining awareness that a certain problem exists, we delay in taking action, which might worsen the situation.

It may be a health, relationship, skill or an attitude related issue. If you don't analyze and deal with it now, it may grow into a bigger issue.

Someone I know closely was running into debt. Overspending was the initial problem which he never bothered to fix. This led to the overuse of credit cards and loans to meet his lifestyle expenses. It seemed to be a debt problem. However, the overspending was still there – the root of the problem grew to the extent where he was no longer able to pay off the monthly installments for the issue. In the effort of paying off debts, he worked overtime with increased stress levels. The result was worsening health which became a new and serious problem for him.

Being and doing things on Autopilot keeps us Unaware of what needs to be done

A <u>study</u> by Daniel Gilbert confirms that 46.9% of the time, we are on autopilot. We are not focused on the task at hand or in the present moment, but busy doing "mind wandering", lost in our own thoughts.

We are living like robots just completing tasks one after the other, without being aware and not paying enough attention to our lives. Hence, the problems that need be resolved now are put aside to be taken care of later.

So, what should we do? Practice Mindfulness. Pay adequate attention to everything that's taking place with and around us. Be in present. Practice mindfulness meditation. What you will get? Well. I have experienced amazing results. You can try and test for yourself.

A Few More Thoughts

I really hope that you found the information in this book useful and practical for your various problem situations.

When the problem catches you somewhere down the road, show courage. Look into its face and say, "You are not going to control me!" The initial feeling of panic that you may experience is natural and obvious, but the sooner you take control of the situation, the easier it will be for you to beat it.

The most important thing is to not entertain the thoughts about potential problems because, if we are doing so, we are expecting the problems. Expectation is the most powerful emotion, according to the world famous book **"Secret"** by *Rhonda Byrne*. Take expectations positively as they come. Each problem I have faced has made me a little stronger.

Though we cannot stop problematic situations from happening, we can reduce the likelihood of them occurring.

Keep things simple in life. Aim at finding simple solutions. For example, if you are single, the problem may be that you are not meeting enough people of opposite gender. So, the solution is simple: meet more people.

One of my favorite statements is, "Every problem has a solution. The bigger the problem, the bigger the solution. But, the solution certainly exists."

Good Luck

Happy Living

Hina Siddiqui

HEY!!! LET'S FORM AN EVERLASTING CONNECTION

As a bestselling author, speaker, blogger, and coach, I've discovered that having only one life is too short and precious to limit yourself to a single pursuit. My work keeps me motivated and helping others to motivate themselves is my work. I am a passionate professional who has written four books on Amazon so far and helped many people to transform their lives by showing them that their interests can be pursued by showing them how to do it.

Like many of you, I worked in the corporate world in various positions for more than a decade before I discovered my true passion for writing and coaching others to succeed. My goal is to help you improve your quality of life so that you can live happier and free of unneeded stress. The techniques that I have learned over the years I will eagerly share with you so that your life can be one filled with adventure and happiness on your own terms.

What I Do for You

Once I found and started living my DREAM LFE, my desire to help people achieve what they truly want in life, got more intense. So here I am – to help you live the best of your life in alignment with the BEST VERSION of you.

My passion is to help professionals improve their communications skills, be more effective at work, and maintain the proper balance between their work and home life. The result of my coaching is designed to help you achieve the following;

- Live your DREAMS
- Have an Ecstatic Life
- Improve Performance at Work
- Build Great Relationships
- Develop Your Personal and Professional Goals
- Produce Better Results

I help you achieve your goals in life by providing one-on-one coaching and/or on-site workshops that last either four or eight hours depending on your needs. The sessions are designed to help you improve your professional communication skills, work abilities, personal skills, and business writing so you can reach your career goals easier and faster.

My services are designed to help you get what you want out of life. Everyone has the passion, desire, and determination to achieve what they want, but many do not have the roadmap that leads to success. This is where I come in to help you.

I am passionate about life and I want you to see all the possibilities that are right there in front of you. Let me help you find your path so you can make your life wonderful.

Enough about me. How about you? I would love to hear from you. Shall be too glad if I can help you in any possible way. Please do write to me at hina@authorhina.com.

Visit my Website www.authorhina.com

Let's stay connected.

Happy Living,

Hina Siddiqui

Review Request

You are welcome to leave an Honest Review about your experience of reading this book including what you were inspired by.

Even a small review with one or two sentences shall help in a big way. All you need to do is just click on the link https://www.amazon.com/dp/B01FHP7A7I & leave a customer review.

You can contact me at hinasiddiqui.2016@gmail.com or hina@authorhina.com for any suggestions and ideas for improvement for my future works.

www.ingramcontent.com/pod-product-compliance
Lightning Source LLC
Chambersburg PA
CBHW050800240726
48654CB00008B/565